DR. MARITA KINNEY, MSc.D

SAY IT 'TIL YOU SEE IT

Harnessing the Power of Biblical Affirmations to Create Your Reality

ISBN: 978-1-953760-45-6

Dedication

This book is dedicated to my beloved father, The late Bishop Dr. Westley C. Robinson and my husband Dr. Demoine Kinney. These men are the visionaries who taught me how to build my faith. They both are men of unshakable faith, and I'm blessed to learn from them.

To my God mother, Elect Lady JoAnne Walker, for providing me encourage and love throughout my life. Also for sharing the details with me of my father's last sermon that was preached at her church, Sharon Pentecostal Church of God. That sermon inspired me to write this book.

Table of Contents

Rest in Peace Daddy

Bishop Dr. Westley C. Robinson

INTRODUCTION

Speaking Life into Existence

"In the beginning, God said, 'Let there be light,' and there was light" (Genesis 1:3). With these words, the Creator spoke the universe into existence, showing us the profound power of words to bring forth life, light, and purpose. This act of creation is more than just the beginning of time; it is a demonstration of the power inherent in spoken words—a power that God entrusted to us.

My father, The late Bishop Dr. Westley C. Robinson, understood and lived by this truth. In his last sermon, preached at Sharon Pentecostal Church of God, he shared this message with an urgency that was palpable. He reminded the congregation that our words are not empty sounds but seeds of creation, carrying within them the potential to shape our lives and the world around us. His message was clear: we hold the same power to "speak things into existence," just as God did in Genesis.

This book is not only a tribute to his life and legacy but a continuation of his final lesson. Through the following chapters, we'll explore the spiritual authority we hold when we speak with faith. Scripture guides us in this journey: Mark 11:23 calls us to speak to our mountains, while Romans 4:17 encourages us to call "those things which do not exist as though they did." Each of these verses, along with others, echoes the creative power of words that God modeled in the beginning.

As we journey through these chapters together, I invite you to embrace this vision that my father so passionately preached. Being a visionary, as he was, comes with both pain and reward. The pain of carrying a vision that others may not yet see, and the reward of witnessing that vision come to life. My father left us with the profound reminder that, like our Creator, we can speak life into our own circumstances. We, too, can say, "Let there be," and trust that by faith, it will come to pass.

CHAPTER 1

The Power of Affirmation – Let There Be...

When God spoke, "Let there be light," the universe obeyed. This simple phrase—"Let there be"—carried the creative force of God's intention. It was not a suggestion or a wish; it was an affirmation of faith and authority. Through this declaration, light burst forth from nothingness, and the cosmos took form. Each time God spoke throughout Genesis, creation responded.

We are made in God's image, and because of this, our words hold that same power to affirm, create, and transform. When we declare "Let there be..." over our lives, we are affirming not only our desires but our faith that what we speak will come into existence. This power is not something we must earn; it's an inherent gift, woven into our very being by a Creator who speaks worlds into existence.

The Principle of Affirmation

The act of speaking life through affirmations goes beyond mere positive thinking. Affirmations are declarations of what we believe in faith to be true, even if we cannot yet see it. Hebrews 11:1 reminds us that "faith is the substance of things hoped for, the evidence of things not seen." By affirming, we're aligning our hearts and minds with God's promises, speaking into existence the things we believe are possible through Him.

My father understood this principle deeply. In his life and ministry, he would often say, "Speak what you believe." For him, these weren't idle words; they were foundational truths. He believed that affirming God's promises, even in the face of adversity, had the power to shift reality. As a visionary, he often saw possibilities that were hidden to others. He spoke life, hope, and purpose over himself and those around him, reminding us that our words carry both intention and authority.

Affirming Our Identity and Purpose

One of the most powerful affirmations we can make is to declare who we are in God. Throughout the Bible, we see God affirming His people, calling them by name, and reminding them of their identity and purpose. When Moses doubted himself, God affirmed, "I will be with you" (Exodus 3:12). When Jeremiah felt unworthy, God said, "Before I formed you in the womb, I knew you" (Jeremiah 1:5). These affirmations were not just comforting words; they were declarations of identity and purpose.

Like God, we, too, can declare our purpose and affirm our identity in Him. Saying "I am a child of God," "I am called," or "I am loved" are affirmations that ground us in the truth of who we are. My father, as a visionary, often encouraged others to affirm these truths about themselves, reminding them that their words had the power to create confidence, purpose, and resilience.

Let There Be: The Creative Power of Words

What do you desire to see in your life? Do you long for peace, healing, purpose, or strength? Begin with "Let there be..." and speak it forth. Let there be peace in your heart. Let there be healing in your body. Let there

3

be purpose in your life. When we affirm these things, we are not only declaring them but giving them room to take root and flourish.

My father's life was a testament to this power. As he faced the challenges of ministry, he would say, "Let there be strength," or "Let there be clarity." He affirmed what he needed with faith, trusting that God would fulfill these declarations. He believed that by speaking these affirmations, he was aligning his heart with God's will, paving the way for these realities to manifest.

Practical Steps to Speak Life

1. **Identify Your Affirmations:** Take time to reflect on what you need or desire in your life. Write down affirmations that align with God's promises and speak to your purpose.

2. **Speak Boldly and Daily:** Incorporate these affirmations into your daily routine. Speak them boldly, with faith that they will come to pass. Remember, affirmations are declarations, not mere wishes.

3. **Anchor in Scripture:** Find verses that reinforce your affirmations. Speaking God's Word over your life brings authority and clarity to your affirmations. For instance, if you're affirming peace, you might declare, "Let the peace of God, which surpasses all understanding, guard my heart and mind" (Philippians 4:7).

4. **Trust the Process:** The power of affirmation is not always immediate; it's a process of aligning your thoughts, actions, and faith. Like a seed, your affirmations need time to grow and bear fruit. Be patient, and trust that what you have spoken will come to pass.

Affirmation as a Legacy

As we speak life into our own situations, we honor the legacy of visionaries who have come before us—those like my father, who taught us to speak boldly and believe fiercely. His last sermon was not only a message but a charge to us all: to recognize the divine power of our words and to carry forward the legacy of speaking life and faith.

In each declaration, we continue this legacy, building a life that reflects the power, purpose, and love of God. By speaking "Let there be," we invite the Creator's hand into every area of our lives, trusting that, in time, we will see His promises fulfilled.

CHAPTER 2

Faith in Action – Bridging Words and Reality

Speaking things into existence begins with our words, but it doesn't end there. Just as God's words in Genesis were accompanied by creative action, our affirmations require us to step out in faith, aligning our actions with the reality we're declaring. In this way, speaking life into our circumstances isn't simply a passive hope—it's an active partnership with God to bring forth what we desire.

My father, Bishop Dr. Westley C. Robinson, often emphasized this connection between words and action. He would say, "Faith without action is just a wish." For him, speaking an affirmation was only the beginning; it was the spark that lit a path for intentional movement forward. He understood that words, though powerful, find their true strength when we act on them with faith.

The Principle of Faith in Action

In James 2:17, we're reminded that "faith by itself, if it does not have works, is dead." Speaking life over our situations calls for us to live out those words in our actions, attitudes, and decisions. Just as a seed requires watering and care to grow, our affirmations require us to nurture them with action. This might mean choosing to respond with love when we're affirming peace, or taking practical steps toward a goal we're speaking into existence.

My father believed that acting in faith was a form of preparation for the blessings God intended to bring. He'd often say, "Prepare for what you've prayed for." When he declared, "Let there be strength," he wouldn't simply wait for strength to come. He would take steps to position himself for strength, perhaps by seeking rest, support, or wisdom. In this way, he modeled a life of active faith—an example that calls us to do the same.

Bridging the Gap Between Vision and Reality

It's one thing to speak words of faith, but it's another to live them out, especially when we don't yet see the results. Speaking "Let there be..." requires courage and perseverance to act in alignment with our vision, to literally *feel* the emotions as if it had come to past. This may mean trusting the process even when we face setbacks or doubts. Remember the story of Abraham, who "believed in the Lord, and He accounted it to him for righteousness" (Genesis 15:6). Abraham's faith was not only in words but in action, moving forward even when the fulfillment of God's promise seemed distant.

To bring our affirmations into reality, we must act as though they are already true and feel it in your spirit. If we're declaring "Let there be peace," our actions should reflect peace. If we're affirming purpose, our steps should reflect intentionality. This is where true transformation begins—not just in words, but in the consistent alignment of our lives with those words.

Practical Ways to Live Out Your Affirmations

1. **Visualize and Plan:** Create a clear mental image of the reality you're speaking into existence. Visualize what it would look like, and begin

planning steps toward it. This act of visualization anchors your faith, bridging the gap between vision and action.

2. **Act with Intention:** Every action, no matter how small, should move you closer to the affirmation you've declared. If you're speaking life into a new career, take practical steps toward that goal, like networking, learning new skills, or seeking guidance.

3. **Persist Through Doubt:** There will be moments of doubt, but persistence is key. Remind yourself of Hebrews 10:23: "Let us hold fast the confession of our hope without wavering, for He who promised is faithful." Faith is the assurance that what we're speaking is already taking shape, even if we can't yet see it.

4. **Celebrate Small Wins:** Progress may come in small steps, but every step is meaningful. Celebrate the small wins along the way, as these moments reinforce your faith and encourage you to keep moving forward.

Faith in Action: My Father's Legacy

My father's life was a testament to faith in action. He would often encourage those around him to live as though their prayers were already answered and to not be afraid to think big. Unfortunately, I didn't truly understand this concept until after he had passed away. One of his favorite scriptures was Mark 11:24, "Whatever you ask for in prayer, believe that you have received it, and it will be yours." This scripture wasn't just a source of comfort; it was a charge to act as if his requests had already been granted.

When he prayed for healing, he acted with the faith that healing was on its way. When he declared strength, he prepared himself mentally and spiritually to receive it. This legacy of faith in action inspires us to be not only speakers of faith but doers of faith. He taught us that living in alignment with our words creates a fertile ground for God's promises to take root.

Let There Be: Stepping Out in Faith

What is God calling you to speak and act upon today? If you're affirming a new season of peace, begin by creating peaceful habits in your day. If you're declaring healing, take steps toward wholeness in every way, whether through prayer, support, or self-care. The journey of faith is one of small steps, each one bringing you closer to the reality you're creating with your words.

As you declare "Let there be..." in your life, remember that faith is active. It moves forward, even when the destination is unclear. This chapter is an invitation to take that step, to partner with God not only in word but in action. As you align your life with your affirmations, you'll find that the things you've spoken will begin to manifest—not as sudden miracles, but as the unfolding of God's faithfulness.

CHAPTER 3

The Resilience of Faith – Sustaining Your Words

Speaking life and stepping out in faith are powerful actions, but they are often met with challenges and delays that test the strength of our resolve. When we declare "Let there be…" over our lives, we must be prepared for moments when our faith is stretched thin, when the reality we hope for feels distant, or when obstacles arise that threaten to silence our affirmations. It is in these moments that resilience becomes essential.

The Test of Time and Trials

Faith is not only revealed in our words or initial steps but in how we endure the journey. The Bible is filled with examples of resilience in the face of waiting and adversity. Abraham waited years for the promise of a son, and Joseph endured betrayal and imprisonment before his dream of leadership came true. These stories teach us that speaking and believing must be accompanied by resilience—the determination to hold on, even when circumstances seem contradictory.

James 1:2-4 encourages us, "Count it all joy when you fall into various trials, knowing that the testing of your faith produces patience. But let patience have its perfect work, that you may be perfect and complete, lacking nothing." Trials are not meant to break us but to strengthen us, ensuring that when our words manifest, we are prepared to receive and sustain them.

My Father's Unwavering Resilience

My father's life was marked by resilience. He endured a lot silently. As I child I could sense when he was in the middle of a storm, but it was intuitive because he didn't show it outwardly. He remained optimistic and was a very positive thinker. I used to think that kind of thinking was weird and unrealistic. Those lessons were extremely hard to grasp as a child. He understood that affirmations and actions are sometimes met with resistance, whether through circumstances, doubt, or even opposition from others. Yet he would remind those around him, "Don't let delay be mistaken for denial." He taught that God's timing is perfect, even when it does not align with our expectations.

I remember a time when my father faced a particularly difficult season in his ministry. I was in the first grade and he had a stroke and could no longer walk. The vision he had spoken over his life seemed impossible, with setbacks at every turn. He used to tell me that he was going to walk again, yet I would watch him bed ridden. I used to cry because I desperately wanted to believe him. However, as nearly two years passed, I had lost faith and accepted what seemed to be our new reality. Yet, instead of retreating, he pressed on, reaffirming his words daily without wavering in his faith. His resilience was his testimony, proving that the true test of faith is in holding fast to our declarations when we can't yet see their fulfillment. Watching my father not give up on learning to walk again, was priceless. He saw himself walking, he told people that he was going to walk again, although I could see the doubt in their eyes. But he proved the doctors and spectators wrong. After two long years, he was walking again. That was the first time I witnessed true faith.

Nurturing Resilience in Your Journey

1. **Stay Anchored in the Word:** Scripture is our anchor in moments of doubt. When your resilience is tested, turn to verses that reaffirm God's promises. Isaiah 40:31 reminds us, "But those who wait on the Lord shall renew their strength; they shall mount up with wings like eagles." Meditating on such verses can strengthen your resolve when your journey feels long.

2. **Surround Yourself with Encouragement:** Resilience is nurtured in a supportive environment. My father would often say, "Surround yourself with people who speak life." Seek out those who remind you of your affirmations, encourage you in moments of doubt, and stand with you in faith.

3. **Practice Gratitude:** Gratitude shifts our focus from what we lack to what we have. In moments of waiting, find things to be thankful

for. This practice can help sustain your faith and remind you that progress is still happening, even if it's unseen. 1 Thessalonians 5:18 advises, "In everything give thanks; for this is the will of God in Christ Jesus for you."

4. **Reaffirm and Adjust:** Resilience does not mean rigidity. There may be times when you need to adjust your approach without abandoning your affirmation. Be flexible, and trust that God is guiding you even when He redirects your path.

Overcoming the Voices of Doubt

One of the greatest challenges to resilience is the voice of doubt, whether it comes from within or from those around us. My father believed that doubt was the enemy of faith and resilience. He would often repeat, "Guard your heart and mind." When negative thoughts arise, counter them with the truth of your affirmations and the promises of God.

Jesus set an example of resilience in the face of doubt and opposition. When faced with disbelief, He continued to speak and act in faith. Mark 6:5-6 tells us that even when His message was met with unbelief in

His hometown, He did not waver. This resilience is what we are called to embody when our affirmations are met with skepticism.

"Let There Be" Through Seasons of Waiting

The declaration "Let there be…" is not a one-time act; it's a continuous posture of faith. Seasons of waiting are opportunities to grow stronger, to deepen our trust, and to prepare ourselves for what we are speaking into existence. Resilience is the bridge that carries us from the initial declaration to the fulfillment of our words.

When my father stood before his congregation for the last time, delivering his final sermon, he did so as a man who had spoken countless affirmations, acted upon them, and endured the wait with unwavering resilience. He taught us that true faith is not only in saying, "Let there be," but in holding onto that declaration when the journey becomes difficult. His life was a testament that resilience brings forth the rewards of spoken faith.

Your Call to Resilience

As you continue to declare life over your circumstances, remember that resilience is your strength. Hold fast to your words, align your actions, and trust that God is faithful to complete the work He has started. When doubts rise or delays occur, let them be reminders not of the impossibility but of the importance of perseverance.

Speak, act, and remain resilient, for the words you have declared will find their way to fulfillment. Just as my father preached and lived, may you hold onto your "Let there be…" with the confidence that the One who promised is faithful.

CHAPTER 4

Speaking Life into the Impossible

In life, we are often faced with situations that appear insurmountable—moments when hope seems lost, and the promises we've spoken feel distant or even impossible. Yet it is in these moments that the power of our words and unwavering faith are most crucial. The story of Ezekiel and the valley of dry bones (Ezekiel 37:1-10) is one of the clearest biblical examples of speaking life into what seems hopeless. It's a reminder that even in the most desolate places, our words can bring life, hope, and transformation.

Ezekiel's Vision: The Power of Prophetic Declaration

Ezekiel found himself standing in a valley filled with dry, lifeless bones—a scene that symbolized death and hopelessness. God's command was simple yet profound: "Prophesy to these bones and say to them, 'Dry bones, hear the word of the Lord!'" (Ezekiel 37:4). The prophet spoke as instructed, and as he declared life over the bones, they began to come together, sinews forming and breath entering them, transforming death into an army of life.

This story illustrates the incredible power of speaking life into seemingly impossible situations. The moment Ezekiel opened his mouth and spoke God's words, the impossible became possible. This is the power we hold when we speak with faith. He believed that when we speak life, we invite God's intervention and open the door for miracles.

Declaring Life Over Dead Situations

We all have our "valleys of dry bones"—places in our lives that seem devoid of hope or possibility. It might be a dream that feels unreachable, a relationship that appears broken beyond repair, or a situation that seems destined to fail. Speaking life over these circumstances is not about ignoring reality; it's about acknowledging a higher truth. As believers, we know that God can breathe life into what seems dead and hopeless.

My father's life was marked by moments when he spoke over the impossible. One such moment was when we faced a financial crisis. As a full time minister, he had to have faith that we would be taken care of. While others would have worried and doubted, he stood and declared, everyone that God was our provider and we would not go without. "Let there be provision." He reminded us that God's resources are limitless, and he spoke faith into that seemingly hopeless situation. In the weeks that followed, unexpected support came through. I can still remember him having no other choice, but to trust God. Although fear was trying to overtake him, he wouldn't give in.

How to Speak Life Over the Impossible

1. **Acknowledge the Reality but Declare a Greater Truth:** Ezekiel saw the bones for what they

were—dry and lifeless. He didn't ignore the situation, but he spoke God's word over it. When we face our valleys, we must acknowledge our reality but declare God's promises over it. For example, if you're facing a health crisis, acknowledge it but declare, "By His stripes, I am healed" (Isaiah 53:5).

2. **Speak with Authority:** When God instructed Ezekiel, He didn't say, "Ask the bones if they want to live." He said, "Prophesy to these bones." Speaking life over the impossible requires boldness and authority. Remember that God has given you the power to declare His will with confidence. My father often encouraged his congregation to "speak with the authority of heaven," knowing that their words carried divine power.

3. **Partner Your Words with Faith:** Speaking life is more than just words; it's the belief that accompanies them. Mark 11:24 says, "Whatever you ask for in prayer, believe that you have received it, and it will be yours." When you declare life over an impossible situation,

23

believe that your words are already setting change into motion.

4. **Persist in Your Declaration:** There may be times when speaking life over a situation does not yield immediate results. Persistence is key. Just as Ezekiel continued to prophesy until the full transformation occurred, we must continue to speak life over our valleys until we see the manifestation. My father exemplified this persistence, often repeating his affirmations of faith until breakthroughs came.

Testimonies of Speaking Life

My father's life was filled with moments where speaking life transformed the impossible into reality. My father would lay hands on people, and declared healing with the simple words, praying for health and restoration. Though the journey was difficult, he would help to encourage people to believe in the power of their words, using his own healing testimony as proof of God healing power. Crediting the faith-filled words spoken over his life. This became a cornerstone testimony in his ministry, reinforcing the power of speaking life.

Your Valley, Your Voice

What is your valley of dry bones? It might be a dream that you've given up on, a relationship that has fractured, or a situation that seems beyond saving. I encourage you to look at it with the eyes of faith and speak life over it. Declare, "Let there be hope," "Let there be healing," "Let there be restoration." Your words, paired with faith, invite the breath of God to move in your life.

As you speak life, know that you are following in the footsteps of visionaries like my father, who understood that even in the darkest valleys, the power of life and death lies in the tongue (Proverbs 18:21). When we choose to speak life, we choose to invite the God of the impossible into our reality.

CHAPTER 5

Overcoming Doubt – The Battle for Your Words

Every time we declare "Let there be…" over our lives, we are making a statement of faith. Yet, even the most resilient believers encounter moments of doubt—those whispers in the dark that question whether what we are speaking will ever come to pass. Doubt is not a new struggle; it's a battle that has existed since the beginning. Even those who walked closely with God, like Moses and the disciples, experienced moments of wavering faith. The key lies in how we respond to these moments and continue to speak life despite them.

The Reality of Doubt

Doubt often arises in the space between speaking and seeing. It's easy to proclaim "Let there be..." when faith is strong, and the future looks promising. But what happens when time passes and the reality we've declared seems distant or impossible? This is when doubt begins to creep in, attempting to replace our bold affirmations with uncertainty.

In Matthew 14:29-31, we see Peter walking on water toward Jesus, defying the laws of nature by faith alone. But when he noticed the wind and the waves, doubt took hold, and he began to sink. Jesus caught him and said, "You of little faith, why did you doubt?" This moment captures the battle we face when we take bold steps of faith but then get distracted by the storms around us.

My father knew that doubt was one of the greatest challenges to faith. He would often tell his congregation, "Doubt is a thief—it steals your words before they can bear fruit." He believed that while doubt was natural, it didn't have to be fatal to our faith. His advice was always to confront doubt head-on and replace it with truth.

Practical Steps to Overcome Doubt

1. **Acknowledge It Without Accepting It:** It's important to recognize when doubt arises but not to accept it as truth. Doubt may come, but it does not have to stay. Acknowledging your doubt allows you to confront it directly without letting it take root in your heart.

2. **Replace Doubt with Truth:** When doubt begins to whisper, respond with the truth of God's promises. Use scripture as a weapon against doubt. When you start to feel uncertain, declare verses like Mark 9:23, "Everything is possible for one who believes," to reaffirm your faith and realign your thoughts.

3. **Reflect on Past Victories:** My father often advised, "Look back at what God has already done." Remembering past moments when God came through despite uncertainty can help strengthen your faith in the present. Reflect on your own testimonies and those of others to remind yourself that God is faithful.

4. **Surround Yourself with Faith Builders:** Being around people who speak life and reinforce

your faith can make a significant difference when you're battling doubt. Just as my father would encourage the church to be a place of life-giving words, seek out relationships that do the same.

5. **Speak Louder than Your Doubt:** When doubt becomes overwhelming, respond by declaring your affirmations louder. My father's advice, "Speak louder than your doubt," was not just metaphorical. He meant it literally—raise your voice and declare, "Let there be…" with confidence. This act of vocal affirmation can help drown out the voice of doubt and reinforce your belief.

The Battle Is in the Mind

The battlefield for doubt is often in the mind, where thoughts swirl and questions arise. The apostle Paul wrote in 2 Corinthians 10:5, "We demolish arguments and every pretension that sets itself up against the knowledge of God, and we take captive every thought to make it obedient to Christ." This verse serves as a reminder that we have the power to control our thoughts and choose which voices we listen to.

When my father faced seasons where doubt threatened to overshadow his declarations, he would pause and realign his mind with the promises of God. "Guard your mind as you would a treasure," he'd say, "because it's where your words are born." He knew that what we meditate on becomes what we speak, and what we speak shapes our reality.

Doubt Is Temporary; Faith Is Eternal

The enemy often tries to make us believe that doubt is a sign of weak faith, but this is not true. Even the strongest believers face moments of doubt. The difference lies in what we do next. Do we allow it to silence us, or do we speak over it with the voice of faith? The story of Thomas, who doubted Jesus' resurrection until he saw Him (John 20:24-29), shows us that doubt does not disqualify us. Jesus did not condemn Thomas for his doubt; instead, He invited him to see and believe.

Your faith journey will include moments of doubt, but these moments can also strengthen your resilience if you choose to speak over them. Declare boldly, "Let there be belief in my heart even when I cannot see."

Stand firm, and remember that doubt is temporary, but faith is eternal.

Continuing the Legacy of Speaking Life

When my father sat in the pulpit and delivered his final sermon, he did so as a man who had faced doubt but never let it conquer him. Although he didn't have the energy to stand, he was determined to preach this life transforming sermon anyway. He knew his time was coming to an end. He was about to receive his total healing in glory. He spoke of the power of our words and reminded everyone that even when we falter, the strength to speak life remains. His life was a testimony to overcoming doubt with declarations of faith, showing us that victory comes not from avoiding doubt but from choosing faith in its presence.

As you speak life into your own situations, know that doubt may come, but it does not have to win. Confront it, replace it with truth, and declare boldly, "Let there be..." Your words, spoken in faith, have the power to transform your reality, even in the face of uncertainty.

CHAPTER 6

The Role of Patience and Waiting – Trusting in God's Timing

One of the most challenging aspects of speaking life into existence is the waiting period. After declaring "Let there be…" and taking steps of faith, there often comes a time when it feels like nothing is happening. This is the period when patience is tested, and faith must be anchored deeply in God's timing.

The Waiting Period: A Season of Growth

Waiting is not just a passive state but an active season of growth and preparation. In the Bible, there are countless stories of those who had to wait for the fulfillment of God's promises. Abraham waited for the birth of Isaac, Joseph endured years of hardship before becoming a leader in Egypt, and David spent years fleeing from Saul before he was crowned king. Each of these seasons was marked by patience and trust in God's timing.

Isaiah 40:31 reminds us, "But those who wait on the Lord shall renew their strength; they shall mount up with wings like eagles, they shall run and not be weary, they shall walk and not faint." This verse is not just a promise of endurance but a reminder that waiting on God renews and strengthens us.

Embracing Patience with Faith

Patience is not passive; it is an active demonstration of faith. While waiting, our actions, thoughts, and words should continue to align with the declaration we've made. James 5:7-8 encourages us, "Be patient, then, brothers and sisters, until the Lord's coming. See how the farmer waits for the land to yield its valuable crop, patiently waiting for the autumn and spring rains. You too, be patient and stand firm."

Farmers plant seeds and tend to their crops while waiting for the harvest. They do not doubt that the harvest will come, even when they cannot see growth immediately. In the same way, when we speak "Let there be..." over our lives, we must continue nurturing our faith and actions as we wait.

Practical Ways to Embrace Patience

1. **Stay in Prayer:** The waiting period is a powerful time to deepen your relationship with God. My father always emphasized that prayer is not just about asking but about aligning our will with God's and listening for His guidance. Spend time in prayer, asking for patience and wisdom while you wait.

2. **Focus on Preparation:** Use the waiting period to prepare for what you've declared. If you've spoken life over a new career opportunity, take courses, build your skills, or network with others in your field. Preparation during the waiting period is an act of faith that shows you believe your words will manifest.

3. **Maintain Your Declaration:** Continue to speak life and affirm your declaration. Don't let the passage of time cause your voice to grow silent.

My father would remind the congregation, "Just because you don't see it yet doesn't mean it's not on the way."

4. **Find Joy in the Present:** Waiting can be difficult, but finding moments of joy and gratitude in the present helps sustain patience. Reflect on the blessings you currently have, and be grateful for the journey, not just the destination. 1 Thessalonians 5:16-18 advises, "Rejoice always, pray continually, give thanks in all circumstances; for this is God's will for you in Christ Jesus."

The Blessing in the Wait

The story of Joseph is a perfect example of the blessing that can be found in waiting. Sold into slavery by his brothers, wrongfully imprisoned, and forgotten, Joseph endured years of waiting before seeing the fulfillment of his dreams. Yet, when the time came, he rose to a position of power that allowed him to save not only Egypt but his own family. What seemed like a delay was actually God's divine timing, positioning Joseph for a greater purpose than he could have imagined.

My father would often say, "Delay is not denial; it is divine timing." This teaching encouraged many who felt discouraged by waiting, reminding them that the delay was not without purpose. In those moments of waiting, God was working behind the scenes, aligning circumstances, people, and opportunities that would come together at the right time.

Trusting God's Timing

Trusting God's timing means believing that He knows when we are ready to receive what we have spoken. It is an act of surrender, acknowledging that while we have the power to declare "Let there be…," God determines the season in which it will come to pass. Ecclesiastes 3:1 tells us, "To everything there is a season, a time for every purpose under heaven."

As you speak life and wait for its fulfillment, remember that patience is not just a test but a tool. It molds you, strengthens you, and prepares you to receive the blessings you have declared. Like my father, speak with conviction, wait with faith, and trust that in the silence, God is still at work. The time will come when what you have declared will break through, and you will see the fruit of your patience and perseverance.

CHAPTER 7

Speaking Life Over Others – The Ripple Effect of Your Words

While speaking life into our own circumstances is powerful, the true impact of our words extends far beyond ourselves. The ability to speak life over others is a gift that can transform relationships, build faith, and create a ripple effect of encouragement and hope. In a world that often speaks negativity and doubt, choosing to declare life and hope over the people in our lives is an act of love and faith that mirrors the teachings of Jesus.

The Biblical Call to Speak Life Over Others

Throughout scripture, we are reminded of the importance of building each other up with our words.

Ephesians 4:29 urges us, "Do not let any unwholesome talk come out of your mouths, but only what is helpful for building others up according to their needs, that it may benefit those who listen." Our words have the power to uplift, inspire, and bring life to those who may be struggling.

Jesus set the ultimate example of speaking life over others. In moments of doubt and fear, He spoke peace and assurance. To the woman caught in adultery, He said, "Neither do I condemn you; go and sin no more" (John 8:11), offering her a new beginning. To His disciples, He spoke words of courage: "Peace I leave with you; my peace I give you" (John 14:27). These words not only calmed their fears but empowered them to continue His work after His departure.

My father was known for speaking life over others. Whether it was a congregation member going through a difficult time or a friend facing doubt, he had a way of using his words to breathe hope and encouragement. One of his favorite phrases was, "Your miracle is on the way," a simple yet profound statement that made those he spoke to feel valued and capable.

I remember one specific instance when my brother Westley faced a personal crisis, he was in jail. Feeling lost and burdened, he was getting tired of the consequences of being out in the streets. My father always showed compassion. Someone was trying to test my father's faith by ask how my brother was doing. Wanting to see if my father would say anything negative regarding the situation. Instead he smiled, and then said, "Thank you for asking, my son is currently getting his testimony." My father refused to say anything that wouldn't speak life into my brother's situation. Those words, spoken with conviction, marked the beginning of my faith. I believed in my heart that my brother's journey to rebuilding his life was possible. Years later, my brother began to make better decisions after having his children. I witnessed his mind shifting towards his true identity of greatness. Unfortunately, his previous lifestyle caught up with him and claimed his life. (RIP Westley).

The Impact of Speaking Life Over Others

When we choose to speak life over others, we become vessels of God's love and encouragement. Proverbs 16:24 reminds us, "Gracious words are a honeycomb, sweet to the soul and healing to the bones." The words we choose can bring comfort to the weary, joy to the disheartened, and strength to the weak.

Speaking life over others doesn't require grand gestures; it can be as simple as reminding someone of their worth, declaring hope over their challenges, or speaking peace into their storm. My father taught that "Words are seeds—plant them wisely." The seeds we plant in others can yield a harvest of faith, resilience, and transformation.

Practical Ways to Speak Life Over Others

1. **Affirm Their Value:** Remind people of their inherent worth. Use phrases like "You are loved," "You are capable," or "You are chosen by God." These reminders can shift a person's perspective and encourage them in moments of doubt.

2. **Speak Encouragement During Trials:** When someone is going through a tough time, speak words that instill hope. Instead of focusing on the difficulty, remind them of God's faithfulness. Say things like, "God is with you in

this, and He will see you through," or "Let there be strength and perseverance as you face this challenge."

3. **Acknowledge Growth and Progress:** Celebrate the small victories in others' lives and remind them of their progress. Even if they haven't reached their final goal, affirming the steps they've taken can be powerful. Say, "I see how far you've come, and I am proud of you," or "Keep going; you are closer than you think."

4. **Pray and Prophesy Over Them:** If someone is comfortable with it, pray with them and declare God's promises over their life. My father often encouraged people by praying aloud and speaking blessings over them, declaring, "Let there be peace, healing, and joy in your life."

The Ripple Effect of Your Words

One of the most beautiful aspects of speaking life over others is that it creates a ripple effect. When you sow words of life, they often inspire those who receive them to do the same for others. Imagine a world where more people spoke encouragement, hope, and love. It begins with one voice—yours.

My father's legacy of speaking life still echoes through the lives of those he touched. People who were once uplifted by his words have gone on to encourage others, passing on that gift of life-giving language. It's a reminder that the words we speak don't just impact the moment; they can create a legacy that outlives us.

Your Voice, Their Hope

As you continue to speak life into your own circumstances, remember to extend that power to those around you. Your words may be the very thing that helps someone hold on a little longer, step forward in faith, or believe that they are capable of more. Speak boldly, speak kindly, and most of all, speak life.

When you declare, "Let there be…" over someone else's life, you are inviting God's presence into their situation and showing them that they are not alone. The power of your words, paired with faith, can transform not only your life but the lives of those around you.

CHAPTER 8

The Role of Community Support – Amplifying Your Voice of Faith

While the journey of speaking life begins with individual faith and declarations, it is magnified and sustained through the power of community. Being surrounded by others who share your beliefs, encourage you, and speak life into your situation can make all the difference. The Bible reminds us in Ecclesiastes 4:9-10, "Two are better than one, because they have a good return for their labor: If either of them falls down, one can help the other up." A supportive community helps reinforce your faith, lifts you during times of doubt, and joins you in your declarations.

Community as a Source of Strength

Throughout scripture, we see examples of the power of community and collective faith. The early church in Acts 2:42-47 was a testament to how believers, when gathered together in unity, could see miracles, share resources, and strengthen each other's faith. This communal support amplified their ability to face persecution, spread the Gospel, and maintain hope during difficult times.

The Power of Unified Declarations

When a group of people speaks life together, it creates a powerful atmosphere where faith is strengthened, and God's presence is invited in a unique way. Jesus said in Matthew 18:20, "For where two or three gather in my name, there am I with them." This promise underscores the impact that community has in amplifying faith.

I remember gatherings where my father would lead the congregation in declaring life over shared challenges. Whether it was praying for a member facing illness, seeking breakthrough for financial struggles, or speaking hope over an entire community, the unity in those moments was palpable. People left those

45

gatherings with renewed strength, bolstered not just by their own declarations but by the voices of others standing in agreement.

How Community Support Amplifies Faith

1. **Collective Encouragement:** In moments of doubt or discouragement, a supportive community can remind you of the truth you're speaking. Hearing others say, "I believe with you," or "We're standing together in faith," reinforces that you are not alone in your journey.

2. **Prayer Circles and Group Declarations:** Joining or forming prayer circles where you collectively declare God's promises over each other can be a powerful way to amplify your faith. Speaking life in a group setting allows faith to build and strengthen among the members, creating an atmosphere where belief can flourish.

3. **Sharing Testimonies:** Hearing stories of others who have seen the fruit of their declarations can inspire and build your own faith. My father loved testimonies, often inviting people to

share how God moved in their lives after they spoke life over their situations. These moments were not just celebrations; they were affirmations that speaking life works and that God is faithful.

4. **Accountability and Support:** Being part of a faith-based community provides accountability. It's easy to falter in your declarations when you're on your own, but having people who check in on you, pray for you, and remind you of your affirmations helps maintain your focus and commitment.

Building Your Community of Faith

If you don't already have a strong faith community, consider taking steps to build or join one. This might be a church, a small group, a prayer circle, or even a close group of friends or family members who believe in the power of speaking life. Here are a few practical ways to engage with or build a supportive community:

- **Join or Start a Prayer Group:** Find or create a group where you can regularly come together to speak life, pray, and encourage each other.

This could be as simple as a weekly online meeting or a monthly gathering at someone's home.

- **Connect with Faith Mentors:** Seek out individuals who have experience with speaking life and strong faith. Learning from those who have walked the path before you can provide wisdom and encouragement.

- **Engage in Service:** Serving with others in faith-based activities can help you form bonds and create a network of support. These connections often lead to deeper relationships where people naturally speak life over each other's lives.

- **Share Your Own Journey:** Don't be afraid to share your experiences with speaking life, both successes and struggles. Vulnerability can strengthen your connection with others and inspire them to open up and join you in your declarations.

The Power of Agreement

There is great power in agreement. Matthew 18:19 states, "Again, truly I tell you that if two of you on earth agree about anything they ask for, it will be done for them by my Father in heaven." When your faith aligns with others in agreement, it not only affirms your belief but multiplies the strength of your declaration.

In times of difficulty, having a community that stands with you can mean the difference between wavering in doubt and holding firm in faith. Community provides reinforcement, hope, and a reminder that your voice is part of something larger. It's a chorus of faith that echoes back to you, lifting your spirits and renewing your resolve.

Your Community, Your Foundation

As you continue to speak life over your circumstances, know that a community can serve as your foundation and fortress. It is where you find strength when your voice grows tired, where you receive prayers when your faith wavers, and where you celebrate when the promises of God come to fruition. The journey of speaking life is personal, but it is strengthened through the power of community. Together, your voices create a symphony of faith that reaches far beyond what you could achieve alone.

Seek out your community, speak life into it, and let it speak life into you. As you declare, "Let there be...," remember that you are part of a greater whole—a family of believers who stand together in faith and support, amplifying each other's declarations and echoing the power of God's promises.

CHAPTER 9

The Power of Gratitude – Strengthening Your Affirmations

When we speak life into our circumstances, it's important to remember that faith is not just about declarations; it's about the attitude we carry in our hearts. Gratitude is an essential part of this process. It's easy to thank God after our declarations have come to pass, but the real power lies in expressing gratitude even before we see the results. Gratitude aligns our hearts with faith, reinforces our affirmations, and creates a positive atmosphere that invites God's blessings.

Gratitude as an Act of Faith

Gratitude is more than just a polite response; it's an expression of trust in God's promises. When we say, "Thank You, Lord, for what You are doing and what You will do," we are essentially saying, "I believe that what I have spoken will come to pass, even if I cannot see it yet." This act of faith is powerful. Philippians 4:6-7 reminds us, "Do not be anxious about anything, but in every situation, by prayer and petition, with thanksgiving, present your requests to God. And the peace of God, which transcends all understanding, will guard your hearts and your minds in Christ Jesus."

My father taught that giving thanks while waiting for the fulfillment of a declaration showed God that you trusted His timing and process. It was not uncommon to hear him end a prayer or a declaration with, "And we thank You in advance, Lord, for what You're going to do."

The Link Between Gratitude and Speaking Life

When we speak life over our situations, adding gratitude creates a powerful combination. Gratitude shifts our focus from what we lack to what we already have and what we believe is coming. It reminds us that

God's promises are true and encourages us to keep speaking life, even in moments of doubt or waiting.

Practical Ways to Cultivate Gratitude

1. **Start and End with Thanks:** Begin your declarations with gratitude and end with it. Before saying, "Let there be peace in my life," start with, "Thank You, Lord, for the peace that is already present and the greater peace that is to come." End by affirming your faith: "I thank You in advance for Your faithfulness, And So it is, or I count it done in Jesus Name, Amen".

2. **Keep a Gratitude Journal:** Write down things you are grateful for, both related and unrelated to your declarations. This practice helps maintain a spirit of thankfulness and reinforces your belief in the good that is already present and the good that is to come.

3. **Express Gratitude Out Loud:** Speak your gratitude as part of your daily routine. My father often encouraged people to say, "Thank You, Lord," throughout their day, even when faced with challenges. This practice shifts the

focus from obstacles to blessings and aligns your heart with faith.

4. **Thank God for Progress:** Celebrate and give thanks for small victories. Progress, no matter how small, is still progress. Acknowledging and giving thanks for these moments strengthens your faith and keeps you motivated.

The Spiritual Impact of Gratitude

Gratitude invites peace into your heart and mind, even when you're in the middle of a storm. It creates an atmosphere that pushes back against anxiety and fear. 1 Thessalonians 5:16-18 advises, "Rejoice always, pray continually, give thanks in all circumstances; for this is God's will for you in Christ Jesus." This verse is a reminder that gratitude is not situational—it is a constant, even in difficult times.

When you add gratitude to your declarations, you are not just waiting for something to happen; you are actively preparing your heart and spirit for it. Gratitude reinforces the belief that God is at work, even if you can't see it yet. It reminds you that He has moved before and that He will move again.

One of the most profound lessons my father taught was the importance of thanking God in all things. Even when faced with personal challenges, he would find reasons to be thankful. He would often say, "Lord I thank you and may Your will bed done" This perspective kept him grounded, hopeful, and expectant. His example showed that gratitude was not just a reaction to blessings but a lifestyle that welcomed them.

Your Call to Gratitude

As you speak life into your circumstances, don't forget to infuse your declarations with gratitude. It's more than just a positive mindset—it's an act of faith that invites God's presence into your journey. When you say, "Let there be...," follow it with, "Thank You, Lord, for making it so."

Gratitude is the bridge between speaking life and seeing life. It is the affirmation that while you may not see the answer yet, you trust that it is on its way. Speak life, be thankful, and know that God is working, even in the waiting. Let gratitude be the heartbeat of your faith, reminding you that His promises are true and His timing is perfect.

CHAPTER 10

Dealing with Naysayers and Opposition – Guarding Your Voice of Faith

When you choose to speak life and declare bold affirmations over your circumstances, it's inevitable that you will face opposition. This opposition can come from external sources, such as skeptical friends or family members, or from internal sources, such as doubt and fear. Learning to guard your voice of faith and push past negativity is essential to seeing your declarations come to fruition.

The Reality of Opposition

The moment you step out in faith and declare "Let there be…" over your life, you may find that not everyone around you is supportive. People may question your beliefs, doubt your declarations, or even discourage you from continuing. The story of Nehemiah is an excellent example of dealing with naysayers. When Nehemiah set out to rebuild the walls of Jerusalem, he faced intense opposition from Sanballat, Tobiah, and others who tried to mock and intimidate him (Nehemiah 4:1-3). Despite their attempts, Nehemiah remained focused, saying, "The God of heaven will give us success. We his servants will start rebuilding" (Nehemiah 2:20).

Responding to Naysayers

1. **Stay Focused on Your Vision:** When facing opposition, it's essential to keep your focus on your vision and the words you've spoken. Distractions come to pull your attention away from your purpose. Nehemiah's response to his critics was not to engage in arguments but to continue the work. "I am doing a great work and cannot come down" (Nehemiah 6:3). Take this stance when facing those who seek to undermine your declarations.

2. **Choose Your Inner Circle Wisely:** Surround yourself with people who support and believe

in your vision. My father often said, "Not everyone who smiles at you believes in you." He was intentional about choosing trusted confidants who spoke life and reinforced his faith. These people became his fortress against doubt and negativity. Ensure that your inner circle includes individuals who will remind you of your affirmations and help you stay on track when others attempt to pull you away.

3. **Guard Your Heart and Mind:** Proverbs 4:23 tells us, "Above all else, guard your heart, for everything you do flows from it." When faced with opposition, it's important to guard your thoughts and emotions. Allowing negative words to take root can weaken your resolve and cause you to question your declarations. Instead, choose to meditate on scriptures and words that reinforce your faith. My father would often recite Philippians 4:8, "Whatever is true, whatever is noble, whatever is right... think about such things," to refocus his mind.

4. **Respond with Wisdom, Not Emotion:** When faced with naysayers, it's natural to feel

defensive. However, responding emotionally can lead to arguments and distractions. Instead, respond with wisdom or choose not to respond at all. Silence can sometimes be the most powerful response to those who seek to undermine your faith. Jesus, when mocked and challenged, often responded calmly or chose silence, knowing that His purpose was greater than their words.

The Power of Standing Firm

When you face opposition, standing firm in your declarations is crucial. The story of David and Goliath shows how facing naysayers with unwavering confidence can lead to victory. Before David fought Goliath, his own brother, Eliab, questioned his motives and belittled him (1 Samuel 17:28). Instead of being discouraged, David focused on his declaration of victory, saying, "The Lord who rescued me from the paw of the lion and the paw of the bear will rescue me from the hand of this Philistine" (1 Samuel 17:37). His confidence in God's promise silenced the doubts of those around him and led to a victory that glorified God.

My father faced his share of naysayers, both within and outside of the church. I saw the hurt in disappointment in his eyes. I also remember people looking at my father as if he were crazy when he told people that he would walk again. I'm so happy that he never allowed their negativity to cause him any doubt.

Practical Steps to Overcome Opposition

1. **Affirm Your Declaration Regularly:** Continue to speak your declaration, especially when opposition arises. Reinforcing your words will help you stay committed and confident in the face of doubt.

2. **Seek God's Guidance:** In times of resistance, pray for strength and wisdom. Ask God to help you discern when to speak and when to remain silent. James 1:5 reminds us, "If any of you lacks wisdom, you should ask God, who gives generously to all without finding fault, and it will be given to you."

3. **Find Encouragement in Scripture:** Read stories and verses that remind you of others who stood

firm in their faith despite opposition. Let their examples fuel your determination.

4. **Use Opposition as Motivation:** Let the presence of naysayers serve as motivation to pursue your vision even more fervently. My father often said, "If the enemy is trying this hard to stop you, it's because what you're building is powerful."

Embracing Opposition as Part of the Journey

It's important to remember that opposition is a natural part of any journey of faith. It does not mean that you're off course; often, it's a sign that you're on the right path. Embrace the challenges, stay grounded in your declaration, and know that God equips those He calls. Romans 8:31 reassures us, "If God is for us, who can be against us?"

As you continue to speak life over your circumstances, don't be discouraged by naysayers or setbacks. Hold fast to your faith and remember that the voice of God and the power of your words outweigh any opposition. Like my father, choose to see opposition as an opportunity to strengthen your resolve and deepen your trust in God's promises.

Speak boldly, stand firm, and know that the same God who called you to declare "Let there be..." will also see you through to the fulfillment of those words.

CHAPTER 11

Maintaining Faith Through Setbacks — Navigating the Unexpected

Speaking life and holding onto faith are powerful practices, but what happens when setbacks occur? What do you do when the vision you have declared seems to hit a wall or when progress comes to a sudden halt? Setbacks can shake even the strongest faith, but they are also an opportunity to deepen your trust in God and strengthen your resolve.

Understanding Setbacks as Part of the Journey

Setbacks are not a sign that your declaration has failed. Instead, they are often a part of the journey that shapes your character, builds resilience, and prepares you for the fulfillment of what you've spoken. The story of Joseph provides one of the most compelling examples of maintaining faith through setbacks. Joseph had a vision of leadership and greatness, but before that vision came to pass, he was sold into slavery, falsely accused, and imprisoned. Yet, in every setback, Joseph remained faithful, believing that God was with him. In Genesis 50:20, after years of hardship and eventual triumph, he said, "You intended to harm me, but God intended it for good to accomplish what is now being done, the saving of many lives."

My father, Bishop Dr. Westley C. Robinson, would often remind us, "A setback is just a setup for a comeback." He believed that each setback carried within it the potential for greater victory. He taught me that when you face unexpected challenges, you must hold fast to your declarations and trust that God is using the delay or difficulty for a purpose greater than you can see.

Holding Onto Faith in Difficult Moments

It's natural to feel discouraged when you encounter setbacks. The initial reaction may be doubt, frustration, or even questioning whether your declaration was right to begin with. However, maintaining faith requires looking beyond the present moment and trusting in the bigger picture that God is painting.

Practical Ways to Stay Steadfast During Setbacks

1. **Revisit Your Why:** Remind yourself why you made your declaration in the first place. Reconnecting with the purpose behind your words can reignite your passion and help you stay focused, even when progress is slow.

2. **Stay Connected to the Source:** When setbacks occur, turn to prayer and scripture for reassurance. Isaiah 41:10 encourages us, "Do not fear, for I am with you; do not be dismayed, for I am your God. I will strengthen you and help you; I will uphold you with my righteous right hand." This reminder can help you anchor yourself in God's promise.

3. **Reflect on Past Victories:** Take a moment to recall previous times when God came through for you, especially when it seemed unlikely. My father would often say, "Remember what God has done, and you'll trust what He's going to

do." Your past victories are proof that setbacks don't have the final word.

4. **Adjust Without Abandoning:** Setbacks sometimes call for adjustments to your plans, but they do not mean abandoning your declaration. Be flexible and willing to pivot if needed while still holding firm to the vision you have spoken. This resilience will keep you moving forward, even if the path looks different than expected.

5. **Find Strength in Community:** Share your challenges with trusted members of your faith community. My father's congregation was a source of strength during difficult times, as people came together to pray, offer encouragement, and remind each other that setbacks were temporary.

The Role of Perseverance

James 1:2-4 tells us, "Consider it pure joy, my brothers and sisters, whenever you face trials of many kinds, because you know that the testing of your faith produces perseverance. Let perseverance finish its work so that you may be mature and complete, not lacking anything." Setbacks test our faith, but they also develop perseverance. This perseverance builds spiritual maturity and prepares us to handle the fulfillment of our declarations with grace and wisdom.

Turning Setbacks into Stepping Stones

The key to overcoming setbacks is seeing them not as stumbling blocks but as stepping stones. Each challenge can push you closer to your goal if you choose to learn from it and keep moving forward. Romans 8:28 reassures us, "And we know that in all things God works for the good of those who love him, who have been called according to his purpose." This truth reminds us that even the setbacks have a purpose and that God is weaving them into His greater plan for our lives.

Your Response Matters

How you respond to setbacks determines whether they will hold you back or propel you forward. Choose to respond with faith, determination, and gratitude. Speak over your setbacks with declarations like, "This is temporary. God is working behind the scenes. I will not be moved."

Remember, setbacks are not the end of your story. They are chapters that build suspense, deepen your character, and set the stage for the breakthrough to come. Stay steadfast, speak life, and trust that what you have declared will come to pass, even if the road to get there has unexpected turns.

CHAPTER 12

Living Out Your Affirmations Daily –
Consistency in Speaking Life

Declaring "Let there be..." is more than just a one-time statement; it's a commitment to a lifestyle of faith, consistency, and intentionality. Living out your affirmations daily is essential to seeing your declarations take root and flourish. The power of speaking life is amplified when it becomes a continuous practice that permeates every part of your day, your thoughts, and your actions.

Consistency is Key

One of the most significant challenges in maintaining faith is staying consistent, especially when life's distractions, doubts, and busyness creep in. The practice of speaking life and living out your affirmations daily is what transforms a simple declaration into a lasting reality. Proverbs 18:21 reminds us, "The tongue has the power of life and death, and those who love it will eat its fruit." This verse emphasizes that the words we speak regularly shape our reality.

The Importance of Routine in Speaking Life

Creating a routine helps integrate speaking life into your daily activities, ensuring that it becomes a natural part of how you live. Establishing habits around your declarations and affirmations can keep your faith strong and your mind focused on the promises you're speaking into existence.

Morning Declarations: Begin your day with spoken affirmations. This sets the tone for your mindset and helps direct your focus toward positivity and faith. Say, "Thank You, Lord, for today. Let there be joy, peace, and purpose in my day. Let there be strength to face any challenge that comes my way."

Midday Reminders: Pause during the day to reinforce your affirmations. This could be as simple as taking a few minutes during lunch to say, "Let there be continued focus, energy, and productivity as I go about my tasks." These short moments of reinforcement help realign your spirit and remind you of the life you're speaking into being.

Evening Reflection: End your day with gratitude and affirmations for tomorrow. Reflect on your progress, celebrate small victories, and speak life over your future. Say, "Thank You for today's blessings, seen and unseen. Let there be rest and renewal as I sleep, and let tomorrow be filled with new opportunities."

Practical Strategies for Daily Affirmations

1. **Create Visual Reminders:** Place sticky notes or cards with affirmations in places you'll see regularly—your bathroom mirror, your car dashboard, or your workspace. These serve as gentle prompts to speak life throughout the day.

2. **Incorporate Affirmations into Your Prayer Time:** Include your declarations as part of your prayer routine. When you speak to God, reaffirm your faith and speak life over your situations. This practice deepens the spiritual

connection between your words and God's promises.

3. **Use Affirmation Alarms:** Set alarms on your phone with labels that remind you to speak life. For example, at 3:00 PM, you could have an alarm that says, "Let there be peace and continued progress."

4. **Speak Life to Others:** As discussed in earlier chapters, speaking life isn't only for yourself. Make a habit of affirming others around you. Saying things like, "You are capable," or "Let there be success in your work," not only lifts others but reinforces the practice of speaking life in your own heart.

Consistency Builds Faith

Consistency in speaking life not only strengthens your faith but also changes the way you perceive challenges and opportunities. The more you practice, the more natural it becomes to choose faith over fear, hope over doubt, and action over hesitation. Psalm 19:14 says, "May these words of my mouth and this meditation of my heart be pleasing in your sight, Lord, my Rock and my Redeemer." This verse is a powerful reminder that daily consistency in speaking life pleases God and aligns us with His will.

Overcoming Challenges to Consistency

There will be days when speaking life feels more difficult—days when circumstances challenge your belief or when you feel too overwhelmed to remember your affirmations. Here are some ways to stay consistent:

- Develop Accountability: Share your affirmations with a trusted friend or family member who can remind you and encourage you to stay on track.

- Embrace Flexibility: If your routine is disrupted, don't be discouraged. Return to your practice as soon as you can, knowing that consistency is built over time, not in a single day.

- Celebrate Progress: Recognize and celebrate when you've been consistent, even if results haven't yet appeared. My father often said, "Faith is built in the quiet moments when you choose to keep going."

Living in the Fulfillment of Your Declarations

As you make speaking life a daily practice, you'll find that your affirmations start to take root and bear fruit. What began as simple declarations will become part of your reality. This transformation comes not only from the power of your words but from the consistency and belief with which you speak them.

Remember, the journey of faith is not just about speaking life in moments of inspiration but about choosing to do so every day, even when it feels ordinary or difficult. Speak, live, and embody your affirmations with steadfastness, knowing that God hears your words and honors your faithfulness.

As you continue this journey, let your daily declarations be a source of hope, strength, and unwavering faith. And with each "Let there be...," know that you are shaping your present and future with the power that God has placed within you.

CHAPTER 13

Embracing the Outcome – Trusting God's Plan

As we journey through speaking life and maintaining faith, it's essential to recognize that the outcome may not always align with our expectations. The final step in speaking life is embracing whatever outcome God provides and trusting that His plan is perfect, even when it doesn't look the way we envisioned. Faith is not only about the declaration; it is about the surrender that comes with trusting God to fulfill His promises in His way and in His time.

Surrendering Control

One of the most challenging aspects of faith is surrendering the desire to control the outcome. We speak life with boldness, expecting results, but it's important to remember that God's perspective is greater than ours. Isaiah 55:8-9 reminds us, "For my thoughts are not your thoughts, neither are your ways my ways," declares the Lord. "As the heavens are higher than the earth, so are my ways higher than your ways and my thoughts than your thoughts."

My father, Bishop Dr. Westley C. Robinson, understood this balance well. He believed that faith was not just in speaking but in accepting that God's plan might unfold in ways we don't expect. This acceptance did not mean abandoning hope or settling for less but trusting that God's wisdom surpasses our understanding.

When the Outcome Looks Different

There were times when my father faced outcomes that didn't align with his initial declarations. One story that stands out is when he was praying for a specific opportunity to expand the church's reach. The project fell through, leaving many feeling disappointed. Instead of viewing it as a failure, he reminded everyone, "If this door closed, it's because God is preparing a better one." Months later, a new, more impactful opportunity arose, one that wouldn't have been possible had the first project succeeded. This taught him and those around him that God's outcomes are always purposeful.

Trusting in God's Timing

God's plan not only differs from ours in outcomes but also in timing. Sometimes we speak life and wait longer than anticipated to see results, while other times, doors open more quickly than expected. Ecclesiastes 3:11 reminds us, "He has made everything beautiful in its time." Embracing God's timing means trusting that delays are not denials but part of His divine plan to prepare us and the circumstances around us.

Practical Ways to Embrace the Outcome

1. **Release Expectations:** While it's essential to speak life with expectation, it's equally important to release those expectations to God. Trust that He knows what is best, even if it differs from your original vision. My father would say, "Expect great things but hold onto

them loosely, so God can shape them into what
He wills."

2. **Look for God's Fingerprints:** When the
   outcome isn't what you expected, look for the
   ways God is still at work. Often, the blessings He
   provides are hidden in the lessons, growth, or
   new opportunities that follow what we see as
   setbacks or changes in direction.

3. **Keep Speaking Life:** Just because an outcome
   differs from your initial vision doesn't mean you
   stop speaking life. Continue declaring God's
   promises, knowing that His plan is unfolding in
   its own perfect way.

4. **Practice Gratitude for the Unexpected:** When
   outcomes take a different path, practice
   gratitude for God's guidance and trust that He
   is leading you to something greater. Say, "Thank
   You, Lord, for what You have done and for what
   You are preparing, even if I don't fully
   understand it now."

Finding Peace in God's Plan

True peace comes from knowing that God is sovereign and that He is weaving all things together for our good (Romans 8:28). This peace allows us to speak life boldly, knowing that even if the path looks different from what we imagined, it is part of a divine design. My father often referenced Psalm 37:5, "Commit your way to the Lord; trust in Him, and He will act." He believed that when we commit our declarations, dreams, and paths to God, He will bring about the outcome that is most aligned with His perfect will.

Surrender as Strength

Surrendering the outcome is not a sign of weakness but a demonstration of profound faith and strength. It shows that your trust in God's wisdom is greater than your need for control. It takes strength to say, "Let there be," and then follow it with, "Your will be done, Lord."

One of the greatest examples of this surrender is found in Jesus' prayer in Gethsemane. Faced with unimaginable suffering, He prayed, "Father, if You are willing, take this cup from me; yet not my will, but Yours be done" (Luke 22:42). This moment shows the ultimate trust in God's plan, even when it meant enduring hardship. It's a reminder that our faith should include not just speaking life but surrendering to the will of God.

Your Journey of Trust

As you continue to speak life over your circumstances, learn to hold your declarations with an open hand, allowing God to shape them according to His plan. Embrace each outcome as part of your journey, whether it aligns with your original vision or not. Trust that God's ways are higher, His timing perfect, and His love unwavering.

End each declaration with the peace that comes from knowing that you have done your part by speaking life, and now God will do His part by directing your path. Trust, surrender, and embrace each step, knowing that the One who called you to speak life is faithful to complete what He has started.

CONCLUSION

The Power of Spoken Legacy

The journey of speaking life, maintaining faith, and embracing God's plan is not just a practice; it is a legacy that transcends time. It is a way of living that acknowledges the power of our words, the depth of our faith, and the sovereignty of God's will. As I reflect on my journey and the lessons imparted by my father, Bishop Dr. Westley C. Robinson, I am reminded of one of the most profound ways he affirmed my destiny from a young age.

Every year, without fail, my father would address my birthday cards or greeting cards to "Evangelist Marita Robinson." He did this when I was a child, and he continued this practice throughout my life. Each time I saw those words, they were more than just a title—

they were a declaration. My father spoke life into me, affirming a path and destiny he believed I was called to walk. Even when I didn't fully understand the weight of those words as a child, they were seeds planted in my spirit, shaping the way I viewed myself and my purpose.

To this day, seeing or remembering those words brings a profound sense of assurance and identity. It was my father's way of saying, "I see you, and I believe in what God has called you to be." This consistent affirmation became a reminder that I was not just speaking life into my circumstances, but life had already been spoken into me.

The Lasting Impact of Affirmation

The power of my father's affirmations illustrates a key truth: what we speak into the lives of others and ourselves has the potential to last beyond moments and create legacies. Just as my father's words became woven into the fabric of my identity, so too can the words we speak become anchors of hope, purpose, and faith for those around us.

When you speak life, you are doing more than just declaring words; you are setting into motion a future that aligns with the promises of God. You are planting seeds that, when nurtured with faith, grow into a strong, unyielding reality. My father's simple act of addressing cards with a title was his way of affirming my future, calling out what he saw in me long before I could fully see it myself.

Speaking Life Beyond Your Own Journey

This story is not just about the power of a father's affirmation to his daughter; it is a reminder to all of us that the words we choose to speak can echo through generations. What legacy are you leaving with your words? How are you affirming the destinies of those around you? Just as my father spoke into my life, you have the power to speak into the lives of your children, loved ones, and even strangers, planting seeds that may bear fruit long after your voice is silent.

A Continued Practice

Even now, I carry forward my father's practice. His affirmations taught me to not only speak life but to also believe in the life spoken over me. It is a cycle of faith that continues, a testimony that our words do not fade away—they live on in the hearts and lives they touch. Whether through writing, declarations, or the simple way I speak to those around me, I strive to pass on the legacy of affirming others with the same conviction and love that my father showed me.

Your Charge

As you finish this book and go forward, remember that speaking life is more than a moment; it is a lifelong commitment. Whether you are declaring "Let there be..." over your own life or affirming the destinies of those around you, do so with the knowledge that your words hold power. Speak boldly, live out your affirmations consistently, and trust that God is shaping your path and the paths of those you touch.

And when the outcomes come—whether they match your original vision or not—embrace them with faith and gratitude, knowing that God's plan is perfect. Continue the cycle of speaking life, and let the legacy of your words be one that resonates, builds, and uplifts for generations to come.

Like my father's simple yet profound gesture of calling me "Evangelist Marita Robinson," may your words be a legacy that others carry forward, a testament to the power of life spoken in faith.